THOMAS CRANE PUBLIC LIBRARY
QUINCY MASS
CITY APPROPRIATION

Nouns

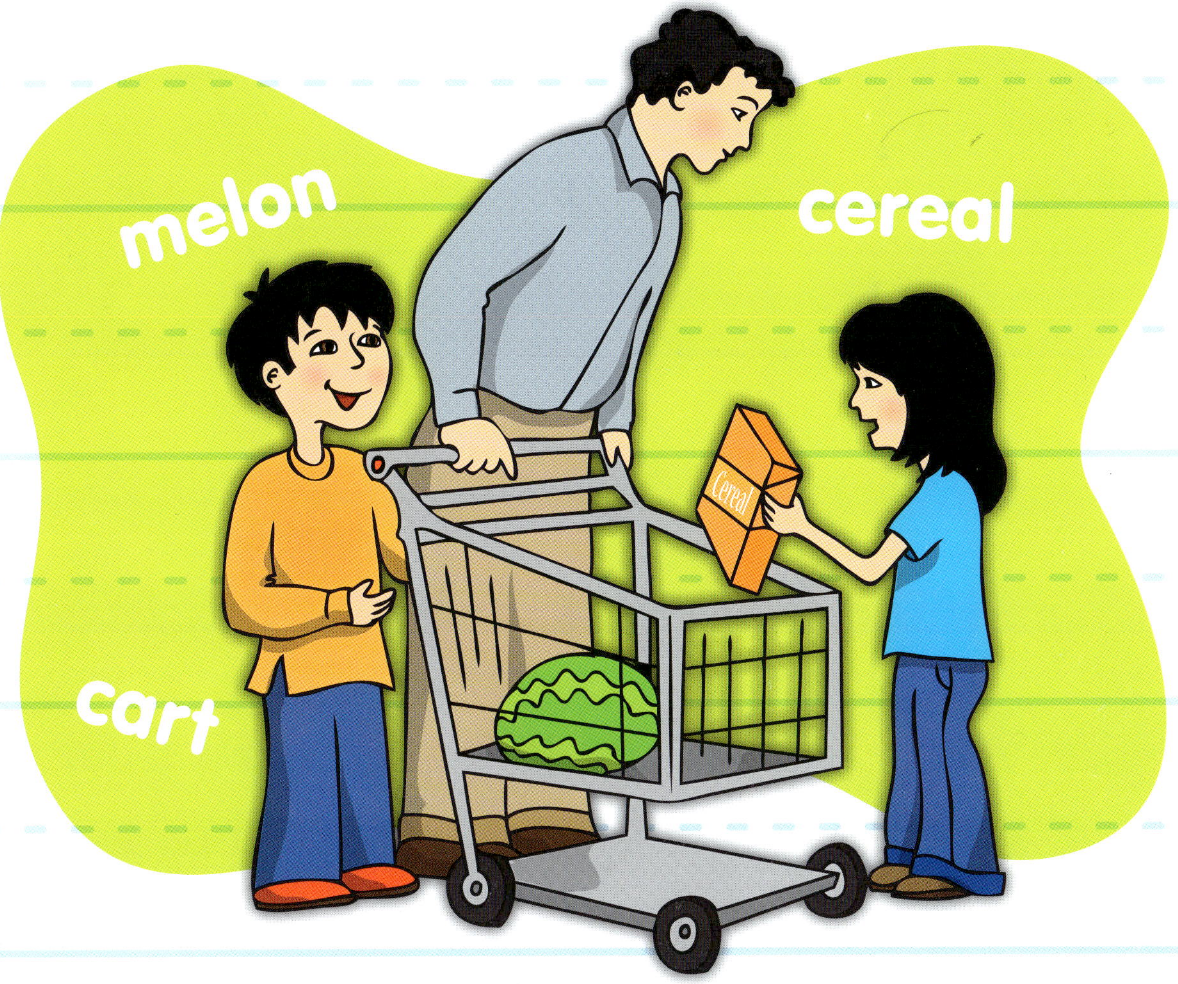

by Josh Gregory

CHERRY LAKE PUBLISHING · ANN ARBOR, MICHIGAN

A note on the text: Certain words are highlighted as examples of nouns.

Bold, colorful words are vocabulary words and can be found in the glossary.

Published in the United States of America by Cherry Lake Publishing
Ann Arbor, Michigan
www.cherrylakepublishing.com

Content Adviser: Lori Helman, PhD, Associate Professor, Department of Curriculum & Instruction, University of Minnesota, Minneapolis, Minnesota

Photo Credits: Pages 4, ©Monkey Business Images/Dreamstime.com; page 7, ©Monkey Business Images/Shutterstock, Inc.; page 9, ©Igor Dutina/Shutterstock, Inc.; page 10, ©liza1979/Shutterstock, Inc.; page 11, ©Frances L Fruit/Shutterstock, Inc.; page 12, ©CandyBox Images/Shutterstock, Inc.; page 18, ©Toniguetta/Dreamstime.com; page 20, ©Pressmaster/Shutterstock, Inc.

Copyright ©2014 by Cherry Lake Publishing
All rights reserved. No part of this book may be reproduced or utilized in any form or by any means without written permission from the publisher.

Library of Congress Cataloging-in-Publication Data
Gregory, Josh.
  Nouns / By Josh Gregory.
     pages cm. — (Language Arts Explorer Junior)
  Includes bibliographical references and index.
  ISBN 978-1-62431-177-2 (lib. bdg.) —
ISBN 978-1-62431-243-4 (e-book) — ISBN 978-1-62431-309-7 (pbk.)
 1. English language—Noun—Juvenile literature. I. Title.
 PE1201.G73 2013
 428.2—dc23   2013005813

Cherry Lake Publishing would like to acknowledge the work of The Partnership for 21st Century Skills. Please visit www.p21.org for more information.

Printed in the United States of America
Corporate Graphics Inc.
July 2013
CLFA13

Table of Contents

CHAPTER ONE
A Long List 4

CHAPTER TWO
More Than One .9

CHAPTER THREE
Getting Proper 16

Glossary 22
For More Information 23
Index 24
About the Author 24

CHAPTER ONE

A Long List

Supermarkets are stocked with a huge variety of tasty things to eat.

Steve and Mia burst through the automatic doors of the supermarket. Their dad pushed the cart behind them. They loved tagging along on the weekly trip to buy groceries.

"What's on the shopping list this week?" asked Mia.

"All kinds of things," their dad answered. "We need some snacks and some **ingredients** for dinners. We also need cleaning supplies, pet food, and a few other things."

Steve and Mia's dad listed the items the family needed. The brother and sister listened carefully. Almost every word on the list was a **noun**. Nouns are words that stand for objects, people, places, animals, and ideas. They are very common parts of speech. You probably say, read, and hear hundreds of nouns every day.

OBJECTS IDEAS PLACES PEOPLE ANIMALS

THINK ABOUT IT

Extra Examples

Nouns can stand for . . .
People: girl, doctor, adult, dad
Animals: dog, lion, bird, deer
Ideas: love, happiness, fun
Objects: table, car, house, wallet
Places: backyard, school, park, store

Steve and Mia's dad pushed the cart into the vegetable section. Steve and Mia followed. "What kind of fruit do you want?" their dad asked.

"Bananas and grapefruits," answered Mia.

"I want berries," Steve replied.

"What kind of berries do you want?" asked their dad. "They have blueberries, raspberries, and strawberries."

Some nouns are more **specific** than others. For example, fruit is a noun. Bananas, grapefruits, and berries are also nouns. They are types of fruit. Blueberries, raspberries, and strawberries are all types of berries.

Choosing fresh, healthy produce is an important part of shopping for groceries.

To get a copy of this activity, visit www.cherrylakepublishing.com/activities.

ACTIVITY

Locate and List!

Locate and list all of the nouns in the following passage:

"We need some cereal," Steve and Mia's dad said. "How about cornflakes?"

"Yuck," said Mia. "I'd rather have raisin bran or granola."

"Shredded wheat is my favorite," said Steve.

"You can each choose one box of cereal," their dad replied. "I'm also going to get some oatmeal. Maybe someone will want a hot breakfast."

"Don't forget the milk!" Mia yelled from down the row.

Answers: cereal, dad, cornflakes, bran, granola, wheat, favorite, box, cereal, oatmeal, breakfast, milk, row. Mia and Steve are also nouns.

CHAPTER TWO

More Than One

"I need to get some vegetables for making chili tonight," said Steve and Mia's dad. "Help me pick them out." He showed Mia and Steve the grocery list. This way they would know what to get.

There are many different ways to make chili.

Bell peppers are sold in several different colors, but they all come from the same kind of plant.

"I'll grab the onions," Steve said as he walked toward the colorful piles of vegetables. "You get the peppers, Mia."

"We need three bell peppers," said their dad. "Get a red one, a green one, and a yellow one. We also need four chili peppers."

Sometimes nouns are **plural**. They are used when there is more than one object, person, animal, place, or idea. Usually, you make a **singular** noun into a plural noun by adding -s to the end.

Steve and Mia's dad looked at the shopping list. "Now we need four squashes for the chili."

"Is this the right kind?" Steve asked as he held up a big yellow squash.

"Perfect," their dad answered.

"How many did we need again?" asked Steve.

"We will need four squashes," said their dad. Some nouns are trickier to turn into plural

Most grocery stores stock a variety of squashes, including green zucchini and yellow squashes.

nouns. They might need an -es at the end instead of just an -s.

"Mia, can you get a loaf of bread while you are over there?" their dad asked. "Actually, make that two loaves, please." Some unusual nouns need different letters to make them plural. For example, some singular nouns end in -f or -fe. The -f or -fe is sometimes changed to -ves when the nouns are plural.

Freshly baked loaves of bread are usually softer than loaves that have been sitting on store shelves.

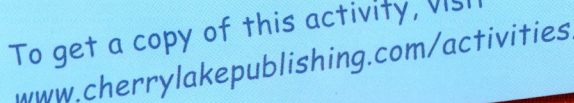
To get a copy of this activity, visit www.cherrylakepublishing.com/activities.

ACTIVITY

Read and Rethink

Read the following passage and change the highlighted singular nouns to make them plural.

"OK," said Steve and Mia's dad. "We still need items for your lunch."
  "I want a snack to pack in my lunch," said Mia.
  "How about a bagel?" their dad suggested.
  "Would a muffin be OK?" Mia asked.
  "Sure," their dad answered. "Would you also like a juice box?"

Answers:
"OK," said Steve and Mia's dad. "We still need items for your lunches."
  "I want snacks to pack in my lunch," said Mia.
  "How about bagels?" their dad suggested.
  "Would muffins be OK?" Mia asked.
  "Sure," their dad answered. "Would you also like juice boxes?"

"The next thing on the list is two fish," said their dad.

"Should both fish be the same kind?" asked Mia. Some nouns stay the same whether they are singular or plural.

"Can we get some cheese?" asked Steve.

"Sure," said their dad.

"Thanks!" said Steve. "I like cheese as much as a mouse does!"

"I love cheese, too," said Mia. "We're both like mice!" Some singular nouns change almost entirely when they become plural.

THINK ABOUT IT

Extra Examples

Here are some types of irregular plural nouns:

	Singular	Plural
If singular ends in -f or -fe, ending sometimes changes to –ves	knife, half	knives, halves
If singular ends with -o, ending sometimes changes to –oes	volcano, potato	volcanoes, potatoes
Some words change a lot	person, tooth	people, teeth
Some words stay the same	deer, sheep	deer, sheep

There are many other types of **irregular** plural nouns. They can be tricky, so keep an eye out for them. One good way to learn which nouns are irregular is to read a lot. Then you will see how different nouns look when they are plural.

CHAPTER THREE

Getting Proper

Names are also nouns. They are used to represent specific people, things, places, ideas, or animals. For example, Mia is a girl and a person. The nouns *girl* and *person* describe Mia. However, the name *Mia* is also a noun. These kinds of nouns are called proper nouns. A proper noun always begins with a capital letter. All other nouns are called common, or normal, nouns. They always begin with lowercase letters.

"Let's go to the pet food aisle now," said their dad. "We need to get some dog food for Sparky." They went around the corner and into the pet food aisle. There they spotted a familiar face.

THINK ABOUT IT

Extra Examples

Here are some types of proper nouns:
Names of people or pets
Names of cities, states, and countries
Names of streets, rivers, lakes, oceans, and other landmarks
Brand names
Names of stores
Titles of books, movies, or songs

Can you think of any other things that have names that must be capitalized?

"Hey, look, Dad," said Steve. "There's my friend Chris from school. Mia knows him, too."

"Go say hi to your friend," said their dad. Steve and Mia hurried down to meet Chris.

"Hey, guys," said Chris. "What are you doing here?"

A candy bar can be a fun treat on a special occasion.

"Getting groceries with our dad," said Steve. "How about you?"

"My brother Joe and I are here with our mom," Chris replied. Just then, another boy walked around the corner. "There's Joe now," said Chris.

To get a copy of this activity, visit www.cherrylakepublishing.com/activities.

ACTIVITY

Read and Rethink!

Read the passage below. Then rewrite it and capitalize all of the proper nouns. Be sure to leave the common nouns in lowercase.

"Hey, chris," said joe, "mom said we can each pick out some candy. I'm going to get a Hershey's bar."
 "What kind should I get?" asked chris.
 "I like twizzlers," said mia.
 "You should get a snickers bar," said steve.
 "There are so many good choices," said chris. "Picking just one is going to be tough!"

What will you buy next time you go grocery shopping?

"Hi, Mom!" Mia said as they walked in the door. "We're back from the store."

"Did you get all of the things we needed?" their mom asked.

"Yeah," said Steve as he carried a bag into the house. "We got plenty of good food to eat."

ACTIVITY

Read and Rethink!

Read the passage below. Then rewrite it and fill in the blanks with nouns you think will work. Be sure to use plural, singular, and proper nouns in the right places.

"I picked out three _____, two _____, and a _____ of _____," said Mia.

"We even got some _____ to drink in the morning," added Steve. "And guess who we saw. It was _____ and his brother _____." Steve and Mia's dog, _____, barked as he greeted them. "We even got some _____ for you, boy," said Steve as he reached down to pet the _____.

"It sounds like you had a great time at the _____," said their mom.

"We sure did!" Mia replied.

To get a copy of this activity, visit www.cherrylakepublishing.com/activities.

Glossary

ingredients (in-GREE-dee-uhnts) items used to make something

irregular (ir-REG-yuh-lur) not following the normal rules or pattern

noun (NOWN) a word that represents an object, person, place, animal, or idea

plural (PLUR-uhl) the form of a word used for two or more of something

singular (SING-gyuh-lur) the form of a word used for just one thing

specific (spuh-SIF-ik) tells you more about something like what kind it is

For More Information

BOOKS

Dahl, Michael. *If You Were a Noun*. Minneapolis: Picture Window Books, 2006.

Pulver, Robin. *Nouns and Verbs Have a Field Day*. New York: Holiday House, 2006.

WEB SITE

Education Place—English
www.eduplace.com/kids/hme/k_5/
Learn more about nouns and other parts of speech while playing games and taking quizzes.

Index

capital letters, 16, 17, 19
common nouns, 16, 19

-es endings, 12

-f endings, 12, 15
-fe endings, 12, 15

irregular plural nouns, 15

lowercase letters, 16, 19

names, 16, 17, 19

-o endings, 15
-oes endings, 15

plural nouns, 10, 11–12, 14, 15, 21
proper nouns, 16, 17, 19, 21

-s endings, 10, 12
sentences, 8, 13, 19, 21
singular nouns, 10, 12, 14, 15, 21
specific nouns, 7, 16

-ves endings, 12, 15

About the Author

Josh Gregory writes and edits books for kids. He lives in Chicago, Illinois.